POURED OUT

POURED OUT

from a place of peaceful waters

Barbie Loflin

WordCrafts

Published by WordCrafts Press
Cody, Wyoming 82414
www.wordcrafts.net

For my mother: my mentor…
Your life has shown me the
True meaning of grace
I am forever grateful
Your God is my God

And Hannah answered...
"...I was pouring out my soul
to the Lord."

~I Samuel 1:15

Contents

Prologue

I Samuel 1:12-15

"And as she continued praying before the Lord, Eli noticed her mouth. Hannah was speaking in her heart; only her lips moved, and her voice was not heard; so Eli thought she was drunk. Eli said to her, How long will you be intoxicated? Put away wine from you. But Hannah answered, 'No, my Lord. I am a woman of a sorrowful spirit, I have drunk neither wine nor strong drink, but...

I was pouring out my soul to the Lord.'"

The words stir my heart as they etch their way onto this page. Poured out. This is how I want to be. This is how I must be if I am to serve Him wholly, love Him fully. For I know there is nothing hidden from His eyes. Though I may choose to withhold myself, I am not hidden. He alone searches my heart and knows me full well. Why not release the deepest parts to Him? Why do I withhold my heart from Him, yet continue to say I love Him? Why do I deny what I feel, hoping to appear more acceptable to Him? He accepted me on Calvary! Nothing I have done or may do can alter that truth. Whether or not I choose to place my faith in that acceptance is a different issue altogether.

Our motives are laid bare before His eyes. The greatest actor the world has to offer cannot mislead Him. The wisest of those who debate cannot convince Him wrong is right. The "great deceiver" was exposed a fraud before His gaze. Why then do we, mere human souls, continue this pretense that all is well in our little world, when inside we feel as if our hearts are being torn from our chests? Why do we smile and simper, "Oh, I'm just fine, bless the Lord," when we really want to fall into someone's arms and cry the pain away; to be held close, not pushed away; comforted, not judged.

We have one such as this. One who will hold and comfort. One who understands and is touched by the "very feeling of our infirmities." We run from the safety of our Father's arms, straight into the torturous fires of the enemy! Even sadder, we do not call for help. We would rather die in our sin or at the very least, suffer great pain and anguish, rather than admit to anyone that we are not perfect Christians and just may need help!

Well, beloved, I bring good news! Jesus already knows! He knows how wretched I am, yet He loves me. He knows there is nothing good in me, so He filled me with His Spirit. He knows I am going to fall—often—and He has promised that His right hand will hold me fast. He knows! He knows! He knows that you have been hurt, and longs to ease your pain. He knows you have been rejected and longs to show you how wonderfully reconciled to Him you are. He knows that you are bound by sickness, so He arises with healing in His wings!

Jesus knows our hearts better than we do. He knows our motives. When we do not know why we do the things we do, Jesus knows. How can we possibly resist One who knows us so completely, and still loves us unconditionally? It does not make sense, but we do it every day. Jesus longs for the deepest intimacy with us and we continue to settle for being mere acquaintances. We crawl beneath the banquet table searching for crumbs, when the table has been prepared just for us and the Lord and Creator of all humanity waits. We spend our lives settling for less than God ever intended. We belong to Him! From the mouth of the Son, came the precious words, "For the Father, Himself, loves you dearly." Dearly! How it must grieve Him when we refuse that priceless love.

This compilation of poems, sonnets, short stories and observations is written from a heart that longs to be poured out before our precious Lord. I feel within myself a deep river, and it is churning like nothing I have known in my lifetime. It pours through me so strongly; at times, I feel there is no way to contain it! I can feel His precious life bubbling through arteries that not so long ago felt dessert-like. He promised rivers, I have found Him faithful to that promise.

Many years ago, because of my complete lack of attentiveness to my Jesus, I entered a spiritual desert. The scariest part of it, in hindsight, was that I did not even recognize the signs. I continued to write Christian music, taught women's classes on spiritual growth, headed up our church Women's Ministry department, and played the piano for our services every time the doors were opened. Works, works, works. My plate was full. Many came to me for advice, most looked up to me. I played the part. Sadly enough, I did not know I was playing.

You see, I believe that sometimes God blesses what we are doing, not because we are in the middle of His will, but because He does not want His innocent children, who might be following along, to be hurt. He basically brings blessing in spite of us. I know this is what He must have done in those years. I pray that no one was hurt by my disobedience to His plan. I pray He kept all safe from this "walking wounded" soul.

I continued my walk, always "doing," but after a very short time I began fighting, then giving in to depression. I wanted to close myself off from everyone and everything. A terrible spirit of heaviness oppressed me.

How foolish we become when blinded by the darkness of our soul.

My disobedience and denial of the truth that I knew deep inside of myself, sent me deeper into spiritual decline. The Truth whispered gently, "you can do all things through Christ who strengthens you, Who infuses you with inner strength, so that you are equal to and ready for all things..." reverberating through my being, while the lie shouted and drowned out everything else. "You are a failure! You will never get control of your life!" Somehow, it is so much easier to believe bad things about ourselves than to believe the good.

I remember thinking, if pride goes before a fall, I must be on my way up! I thought I had no pride. However, in truth I was wallowing in such a great amount of pride, I was unable to reach for the hand of anyone attempting to pull me to safety. Not that there were that many. Remember, I played my part well.

My spirit's voice weakened to the point that the only thing I got when He spoke, was confused. I was floundering. I cried all of the time. No one knew. I smiled, smiled, smiled. "Well, that's just wonderful! Isn't God good?" I would say, while on the inside I was thinking, *I'm just not so sure anymore.* My life was a great deception.

Ironically, even I, who should have known the truth, bought into that lie. I convinced myself that this was just a phase, a time of "testing". Wrong! I had walked out into the middle of this desert, of my own free will; God had not picked me up and placed me there. I had no protection from the elements, my armor was laying somewhere near my dusty old sword of the Word. My food supply, that sweet bread of life, had been discarded long ago, and I was eating dust! I was "deep soul thirsty!"

Still, I just could not figure it out. Denial was my close companion.

Finally, I took a hard look at myself and my situation. I stopped running long enough to really pray. I reluctantly admitted to myself that I had done this. I was not being tested, but instead was living in what I have come to call "disobedience desert."

When God sent the children of Israel into the desert, they had every provision because He had taken them there. God could not have taken me into this barren wasteland because not only was I already scorched and burned, there was no pillar in the sky, and my shoes were worn out from running away from Him. There was no water from the rock, not even a stick with which to hit it. I had to get out of there, and fast! "Help Me, Father!" I cried. I felt His hand take mine and begin to lead me back. Through prayer and fasting I moved forward in my journey out of the dry places, but I still did not understand how I had gotten there in the first place. I mean, I was still "doing" all of the right things, wasn't I?

Nevertheless, just as any good father will do, My Father began His loving correction.

In retrospect I can see that many small decisions led me into a massive desert of disobedience, the main being my failing or refusing to heed the voice of the Holy Spirit when He would speak gently to my spirit. One day He might prompt me to spend time in the Word, or draw away for a little prayer time, only to have me tune Him out or make excuses. He might urge me to have someone pray for me when I was struggling, or prompt me to call someone and just check on them. It was not just one isolated incident; it was a pattern that I had allowed to develop in my life. I only obeyed if it was convenient or something that sounded like fun. If it messed with my schedule or caused me any discomfort, you could basically forget it. *If someone was not going to witness my good deed or even my failure, I was not going to perform. For that was what my Christian walk had truly become. A command performance.* I only performed when absolutely commanded by the circumstance.

It is so sad really. I could remember a time in my life when my greatest pleasure was found in walking beside my Savior, quickly obeying even the quietest whisper of the Holy Spirit. What a waste of life's time to fall away from a Gentle Master such as my Jesus. I still cannot believe I fell so far, and I still struggle at times to grasp what actually happened to me. I gave over to my flesh so often that my spirit man was starving within me. I became stronger and stronger in the flesh and weaker and weaker spiritually. Life became a burden simply because I was trying to do everything my own way. My flesh was carnal, self-seeking, greedy, ravenous, and very lascivious.

Let me tell you right now, the body likes to have its way. When you have been saying yes to all of your little indulgences a.k.a. Sin, for a long period of time, your flesh gets very used to having its way. It should come as no surprise that when you finally get your head on straight and try to regain the spiritual ground you have lost; your flesh is not going to just roll over and say, "Here, let me help you! Yes, I would just love to walk on that treadmill for 45 minutes, and No, I definitely do not want that slice of pie. It will not wake you from your lazy slumber and say, "Let's go spend some time praying and reading the Word!" To the contrary! The first time you are sitting watching television and the Holy Spirit says, "steal away with me," your flesh is going to scream 'Are you crazy? I'm right in the middle of the good part." Or the first time the Holy Spirit says, "set aside some time for prayer and fasting," your flesh says, "Well I can't this week I have two birthday parties and a Women's Advance Dinner—maybe next week. Well, next weeks not good, the Wednesday morning Bible study is having a breakfast..."

Do you see what I am getting at? The flesh absolutely hates the Spirit trying to take the upper hand. It is like two people playing king of the mountain, both trying to get the upper hand. I can tell you without hesitation, Christ Jesus has the upper hand. He can help you bring your flesh into submission to your spirit. It will not be a pleasant thing to your flesh, but I promise you your spirit will flourish beyond measure as you humble yourself under the loving correction of the Holy Spirit. He will complete a marvelous work in us, if we will only make the decision to follow His every prompting, whether great or small.

Now, to continue with my own story...

One day, while cleaning house, a vision began to take form in my mind. I call it a vision, because it was not something I was thinking upon, but was literally dropped into my spirit. I saw myself in the midst of a crowd. Hands were reaching for me, and in each hand was an empty cup. In my arms was a great shiny pitcher. I turned this way and that, pouring from my pitcher, smiling with great benevolence as I poured. The people grasped their cups and turned away, as I poured into each one. They all seemed so very happy at what they had received. However, when I glanced into those same cups, they were empty. I had gone through the motions, offered what I had to those around me, but what I offered had no substance. I looked into the great shiny pitcher and it too, was empty; desert sand gathering at its base. I began to cry out, "Oh, Lord, what have I done!" He spoke to me, His voice that of compassionate correction, "You cannot give what you yourself do not have."

Even now, those words rend my heart. Good intentions are worth nothing in the final analysis. I had given and given and given, trying to earn whatever reward I might receive, but in the process, I had left nothing for my own survival. My coping skills had been spent on helping others cope. In and of myself, I was without resource. *I so wanted others to like me that I had paid too great a price... I no longer liked myself.* I was an empty shell of the person I had once been, and I had given it all away in my quest for earned salvation. Oh what a wondrous blessing to finally realize the absolute no-strings-attached beauty of God's precious grace and redemption.

I very quickly became very uninterested in what others thought of me. I became instantly repulsed by my false behavior. My motives stared at me, nullifying my deeds! I felt true repentance rise up inside of me. You know the kind that puts you on your face, instead of your knees!

The seed of my search for a life "poured out" was implanted at that moment. Labor pains began in the weeks that followed. "I want more of You," I would cry, only to be reminded that less of me would be required. Blessed, difficult, enriching, flesh-defeating, merciful, hard days!

I am learning so much, only to find I am completely ignorant of His ways. I reach a pinnacle only to look over the other side and see I am a mere two inches off ground level. I search the deepest scriptures only to be felled by the gentle words, "For God so loved..." I, like you, am learning as I go, but as I go, this question stirs within me; can I truly be poured out before my Lord?

I know this and little else; I cannot write enough about Him, cannot sing enough praises to Him, cannot for one moment imagine why He loved me enough to give His precious life for me. He fills me so completely when I but allow Him to. All that I will ever be, need, think, feel, hope for, is encompassed wholly in Him.

He is good.

I am not.

I need Him so.

I find it so inadequately put, to say that I am grateful to My Lord! But, grateful, I am. Full-heart, deep-soul, spirit-drenched grateful. I love Him so!

I pray that you are blessed by the prose of my journey. May my soul be poured out before the Lord upon the pages to follow.

POURED OUT

Here I am again, Sweet Lord,
My vessel parched and dry,
Moistened only by the tears,
I have no strength to cry.

My head too heavy Lord to lift,
My feet too sore to stand,
Back fair bent with burdens great,
Holding forth an empty hand.

Rivers of Your life I seek,
Oil enough to fill,
This vessel, then to drench the cups,
Of all who thirst and will.

Springs to wash away the draught,
Fresh rain from Your throne,
Dew so sweet, please wash these feet,
That I may kiss Your own.

Wash away all trace of dust,
Wells of water shout,
Come closer still, Your vessel fill,
For I must be poured out!

Where am I?

It seems I've spent my entire life,
Struggling fierce to be,
Not whom God might think I am,
But someone's idea of me.

I've beat my head against the wall,
Changed my clothes and hair,
Ran, climbed, jumped and cried,
For what was never there.

I thought, I'd surely lost it.
I'd sorely gone down hill.
Must try harder, work, run,
It's just a lack of will.

Oh, I'm just so sick of it.
I'm tired of feeling less
Than what others expect of me,
I never pass their test.

What burden great, to never be,
Found good enough in eyes,
You look to for encouragement,
That now seem to despise.

I want to scream! Get over it!
Can you just love this me?
I'm still the same here in this heart,
But somehow they can't see.

When they look, see surface deep,
Come judgment on my heels,
So easy to be critical,
They don't know how this feels.

Be stronger, take control, you're weak!
It's their 'right' to advise,
But I cannot hear their words,
For the anger in their eyes.

Oh, to be so perfect that,
My only chore might be,
To find the faults of others,
And then tell them what I see.

I'm tired Lord, I've lost myself,
The one that you did make,
Has been overtaken by advice,
I was a fool to take.

Please bring me back Lord, to my mind.
I miss the me I was,
I can't remember her too well,
But I liked her just because...

She knew Your name, and knew her own,
The one that You did call.
Her heart was pure, her walk was sure,
But now she's lost it all.

Find her Lord, teach her true,
To Your opinion seek.
She's crawled too many years of late,
Her knees are getting weak.

11

POURED OUT

Oh, precious Father, help me please,
I want Your daughter here.
The one who held her shoulders back,
And loved free, without fear.

I mere want to be everything,
You created me to be.
So, help me not to worry, Lord,
What others think of me.

I know there's so much more to life,
Than carrying this weight,
Oh promise me, sweet Father dear,
That it is not too late.

"Oh 'tis never too late my child.
For I am still I AM.
Your life is still held in these hands,
And Yes, I have a plan.

You cannot see what I see.
You think that you are lost,
But you are in these arms my love,
And there has been a cost.

Not for your salvation,
But for seeds that you did sew,
I'm holding you to keep you safe,
But child, It's time you know,

You cannot keep on running,
You have to stop awhile,
Find your footing, take your stand,
Take time to laugh and smile.

Works will never get you where,
You long so much to be,
Your destination can be found,
Only when seeking Me.

Lay them down, the burdened words
Close your closet door,
Child, you have to get away,
To find that something more.

Hide away, yes, hide away.
My wings will cover you.
Please, my daughter, run to Me,
For I am calling You.

Answer swift, no time to waste,
Come away with Me.
Here you'll find the Barbie,
I created you to be..."

Let It Go

Sometimes the most frustrating thing in the world can be trying to forget the past. We remember old wounds and unkind words quite easily. It is as if with each replaying of the incident, it becomes etched a bit deeper upon our soul. We hit the rewind button, listen to the whispers of the enemy and fall into the pit of self-pity, crying all the while in our best I-don't-deserve-this martyrs' voice, "Why do you not take this from me, Lord? Why must I continue to wallow in these memories?"

As a child I was forever falling out of trees, off of swings, into ditches, off of bicycles. To say I was not the most feminine flower in the garden would be quite accurate. During all of these "adventures" there were inevitable scrapes, cuts and bruises. I would hobble into my mother's kitchen, hands clenched over the offended area, the first words from my mother's mouth were always, "Come here and let me see what has happened."

Inevitably she would lift me onto the counter and I would open my grimy fingers to reveal the wound. Her next words were "Oh, see, that's not so bad." She would take a soft washcloth, run it under warm water and gently cleanse the area. She would then hold the warm cloth against the wound until it started to feel better. Her final act was to apply a healing balm and seal the wound with a bandage to keep out infection. Her instructions were to leave the bandage on and not to keep opening and closing it. The only time that bandage was to be removed was when mama said so. "You keep opening that bandage up and looking at it and it's gonna get infected."

I do not have to tell you where I'm going with this. The first step in the process is always going to be removing our clenched hands from the wound and letting the Father begin the healing process.

LET IT GO

You carry a wounded heart in hand,
You've done it now for years.
From time to time you take it out,
To mourn and shed your tears.
What should have healed so long ago,
Lays fresh and bleeding still,
For you refuse to lay it down,
Though oft you say you will.
Bound tight by cords of bitterness,
The pain a living thing,
It consumes your days, directs your ways,
Talons in your mind, it clings.
Flashes from your past do play,
You long so to be free,
But, child, you cannot do alone,
What must be done by Me.
Only I can cleanse your mind,
Heal the scars you hide.
Daughter, lay all at My feet.
Forget all you have tried.
Complete and whole, My plan for you,
No ties to wounds of past.
Cease ups and downs, walk stable, sure,
For child, My healing lasts.
Still, one thing will I need of you.
Oh Yes, I'm sure you know.
If I'm to take the hurt away,
You must choose to let it go!

Restoration

The following is a poem for those who have been lost in despair. If you have ever walked in disobedience, given into sins temptation, and found yourself in a place you never thought you could possibly be, read on.

Our God is a loving, faithful God. It is not His will for any of us to suffer or be far away from Him. Unfortunately, we sometimes choose to walk away from His protective hand through disobedience, and find ourselves crying in the dark. Satan loves to come at just that moment and push us over the edge into the abyss. If we are not quick enough to grab the lifeline that God provides, we go tumbling, grasping at whatever looks like it might offer support. Too many times, it is not His comfort we seek, but the comforts that the world has to offer. They are fleeting. We fall a little further and grab onto something else just as fleeting. Compounding the problem is the fact that the further into the pit you fall, the less you see. Things you would have, at one time, avoided like the plague, become "not so bad," if they help you feel better for the moment. But the moment soon passes and you are left alone again.

There was a time in my life that I visited this place where despair dwells. His home was wrapped in beauty that drew me, but once firmly ensconced within his walls, I found myself in dank, decaying darkness, with no visible light. I had accepted the lure, and found myself a prisoner.

When I finally found my way out, with the help of those who truly loved me, I blamed God. Why did He let this happen to me? Why didn't He protect me from the one who sought my life? Then, I began to walk in shame and embarrassment. I built walls inside my heart to help me hide from God. I didn't want to love Him if He was not going to take care of me and cover me. I turned from Him on the inside, but I did not walk away on the outside. I am not sure which is actually worse. For, when everything seems okay on the outside, we can fool everyone—including ourselves.

After a period of time, a lengthy period at that, (for those of you who may need encouragement and have been trying to overcome something in your life for a long period of time), the Lord said, "Enough!" I sat down to work at the computer one day, totally unaware of what the Lord was getting ready to reveal to my heart, and out flowed the words that you will read on the pages that are to follow. He restored me. He covered me. He showed me how He had been there all along. He opened my walled -up heart and made me look inside. He had to. He alone knew what it would take to bring me fully back to Him. He is faithful to do what it takes!

Please allow Him to search you heart as you read *Restoration*, for I can say without a shadow of a doubt that this is truly His plan for all of our lives; to be fully restored to the Father. I have witnessed His handiwork.

He finished what He starts.

RESTORATION

How can I even begin,
to share just what I feel?
How do I reach beyond the false veneer,
exposing what is real?
To be laid out so openly,
before my blinded eyes,
To strip away what others see,
remove this old disguise.

What if I cannot find
the heart that used to lie within?
What if there's no substance,
no victory left to win?
What if I reach oh, so deep,
and find true shallowness?
What if while trying to come clean,
I make a bitter mess?

Somewhere beyond the faith to look,
Lies fear that longs to run,
From things best left in minds recess,
And deeds I'd wish undone.

Can past and present meet
Without true rending of the soul?
Can fragments, pieces, shreds and parts,
When mended make a whole?

What am I looking for?
Why must I undertake this quest?
Would not it be quite prudent,
Lord, to let the sleeping rest?

19

Yes, there are times, when pasts let go,
Forgotten ever be.
But there is a wall I'll not let stand
Between My child and Me.

You hide behind it, think I can't find it,
And often shrink in fear,
But, I've come to tear it down,
Mirror before the face, sweet dear.

You fell away, yes, far away.
You let me down, it's true.
Yet, through it all, My little one,
My love still covered you.

I turned My face away,
My pain was great for you, I wept,
For promises were broken
And the vows you made weren't kept.

You broke before my very eyes,
Lay bruised and bloodied at my feet.
Though I longed to take you in my arms,
Destined appointments you did keep.

You turned your back, My hand went out,
Stayed judgment from your brow,
I turned and cried to angels close,'
We'll help her soon, not now.'

I had to let you go, My love,
For your heart did leave Me first,
You hungered and turned not to Me,
Let others quench your thirst.

Unfaithful each and every deed,
Your heart hardened at My touch.
Through sleepless nights and deep soul fights,
You threw away so much.

Into sins lair, you fairly ran,
So eager to be free,
"No," I called, "Please turn around,
Come running home to Me."

But, even as the words went past My lips,
I knew them lost,
For your course was set, a journey started,
There would be great cost.

You could not see it taking place,
For your eyes were dark as night,
But in heavenlies above
Began the true and earnest fight.

You hang there in the balance,
Each side your soul desired,
But prayers of those who loved you most,
Watered Satan's fire.

Scorched and singed you crawled to shore,
Your piercing cries did start,
But they came mere from your circumstance,
Not a true repentant heart.

Wounds sustained in private battle,
Not so apparent to the eye,
Still stand open, festered, bleeding
At this wall between you and I.

You do not trust Me to keep you sound,
You fear I'll give you up,
You think there's no more water left,
When I've a brimming cup.

You thirst for what you cannot find,
Hunger beyond your grasp,
While before you there's a table spread,
And you have but to ask.

You're mad at Me, you feel I failed,
When you needed Me most.
Yet, in your deepest desperation,
I assure, there was a Host.

I never left you, beloved,
True to the covenant we made,
When as a child, behind closed doors,
Your hand and heart you gave.

I loved you with the deepest love,
Your mind can't comprehend.
I promise you, I have not changed,
Same love now, as then.

Hurt and disappointment
Have followed your steps much,
But I've come to tell you daughter,
I bring the gentle Master's touch.

It's time to come out now, Dear One,
The wall's just in the way.
You've no need to hide,
Come love, abide, in the Father's home today.

Be restored, yes, full and wholly,
No settlement for less.
The battles over, we have won,
Come through another test.

You think you failed this time,
But you will come to understand,
As David did, when sin realized,
You sought the Father's hand.

No, not for gain, or gifts longed for.
Child what you sought instead,
The touch of precious Shepherds hand
Upon the sheep's small head.

Sweet comfort, sweet reunion,
Precious fellowship is found,
When chains are loosed, past cast away,
And fettered hearts unbound.

I love you still.
Be free, in My name.

Commissioned

Have you ever doubted your calling?
Ever thought you just must have just misunderstood?
Ever wish you could get out of your particular placement?

Earnestly remember the calling to which you have been called.
Stir up your gifts.
Be renewed in your faith.

You have been commissioned...

COMMISSIONED

"My hope is fading swift, My Lord,
How can I the standard meet?"
"'Tis not so far to climb, dear child,
When sitting at My feet."

Lofty thoughts soon come to heel,
Troubled minds find rest,
While lying close to hear His heart resound,
"Just do your best."

"But Lord, my best has never been,
Acceptable thus far."
"You've sought the wrong opinions, child.
You are grand just as you are."

"More than I have created,
Child, do not strive to be.
The gifts you have flow easily,
They are a gift from Me.

If what you do seems difficult,
Beyond this peace of mind,
Search your heart for motives true,
Your answers you will find.

For what I've placed within you,
Flows directly from My throne,
The ease with which you translate,
Tells if source be Me alone.

25

So, dear child, let rivers run,
Let My Spirit be swift spread,
Upon the wounded,crying soul,
That you touch in My stead.

Be tendered by emotions,
That at times do overwhelm.
Listen to your Spirits heart,
Discern this soulish realm.

Call white as white and black as black,
No grays your sight will see.
For quite distinctive is the difference,
Between this world and Me.

A counterfeit to meet each circumstance,
You're sure to face.
Look to Me to wisdom grant,
Depend upon My grace.

Speak what you hear and see of Me,
No words from others speak.
Be careful of the sinful pride,
Make sure it's Me you seek.

For much I give into your hands,
My call, a price will pay,
But with it comes greatest reward,
Twill all be yours someday.

For now, though, heart be quite content,
To seek My face and grow.
Patience learn, peace do plant,
Mind all seeds you sow.

Expect the least expected,
For you know not this place.
You've cried for it, fought hard for it,
But never seen a trace.

Surprise, My child, Surprise, I bring,
Your heart wants more, it's true,
But you cannot even fathom,
The plans I have for you!

My thoughts are so much higher,
Than what you could yet perceive,
I ask but small concession,
Daughter you must believe.

Believe Me when the circumstance,
Says this cannot be true.
Believe Me Child, then stand back,
And see what your God can do."

You have been commissioned...

Glimpses

Glimpses of His glory:
Grand display of lightening peels,
Yet, awesome in the way a newborn baby smells and feels.

Glimpses of His glory:
Yes. in universes grand,
Yet, whispered oh so loudly, fingernails on tiny hands.

Glimpses of His glory:
Carving mountains, shaping earth,
Yet, gently, quietly witnessed in the miracle of birth.

Glimpses of His glory:
Angry oceans peaked in rage,
Yet, comfort to the graying head and kind eyes lined with age.

Glimpses of His glory:
Earthquakes devastation rings,
Yet, upon budding branches, a robin's sweet breath heralds Spring.

Glimpses of His glory:
Reigning Judge of nations sin,
Yet, providing seats of mercy, where we,
by grace, begin again.

Further Still

$\mathcal{B}$eth Moore changed my life.

At the time of this writing, she does not know this, but I intend to let her know as soon as possible. Several years ago, I began devouring several of her wonderful Bible studies, beginning with *A Heart Like His.* What an absolutely wonderful, life-changing study. I have never enjoyed a teacher so immensely. If you have not had the profound pleasure of experiencing one of her studies, drop this book right now, and run to the nearest Christian book store. You will not regret one moment of time spent under the tutelage of this remarkable woman of God.

Beth is extremely anointed. I sat in stunned silence as she shared her heart and changed mine in the process. Her poetry brought me to my knees while pointing me to the Fathers blessed feet. She stirred something inside of me that has flowed into all aspects of my walk with Christ.

One particular poem she shares in video, inspired the one you are about to read. The wonderful, "God-part" of the whole thing, was that the Lord had been speaking two words to my spirit for a couple of weeks before I watched this specific lesson. I kept hearing Him whisper 'further still.' I was not sure what it meant, but I was decidedly certain that it was not something I wanted to do, or a place I wanted to go. Therefore, when Beth began her poem entitled "Further Still" I was literally brought to my knees.

I cried for hours following that particular lesson, because I knew my Father was calling me to this place. A place beyond where I had been with Him before. He wanted my complete dependence on Him alone. He wanted all of me.

He wanted more.

He still does.

Come with me to my "Further Still."

Beth, my unknowing mentor, if you should ever pick up this volume, I hope you understand that I want to take nothing away from or add anything to your beautiful journey, only to share the fact that you helped lead me to my own. I am eternally grateful for what you awakened inside this woman's heart!

FURTHER STILL

Just when it started, I don't know,
A whispered voice that bid me go,
Beyond this present comfort hill,
Up to the Mount of Further Still.

So gentle was the call, I found,
Myself compelled to turn around,
Looking to see, can this be real?
Did someone beckon Further Still?

My heart laughed, Lord, surely you jest,
To climb this hill, took near my best.
That mount before me sure will kill.
A gentle smile said "Further Still."

But what, I cried, could possibly be,
Upon that mountain I should see?
A frantic, pounding heart I feel,
At thought of going Further Still.

What if I ascend alone,
Revealing scars as yet unknown?
Will you this broken vessel fill,
There on the mount of Further Still?

All within me bids me, "Go—
Until you journey, you can't know,
Sweet soul release, No bitter pill,
Found when traveling Further Still."

No more whispers, Loud the call!
Swiftly, to my knees I fall.
Bowing low my stubborn will,
Crawling to you Further Still.

Soul in wrenching pain, I cry,
Father, please pass this one by.
His answer plain, "No comfort hill,
Climb this mountain, Further Still."

Just at dawn, clear hearts confess,
At last to see the blessed crest.
Liquid light floods, deep wounds heal,
Upon the rise of Further Still.

"Was worth all, Sweet Father Dear."
"Yes, that's why I brought you here.
You could not see back on that hill,
The vision gained in Further Still."

"Must I go back now?" I said.
"Can I just stay and rest my head?
My empty cup, Lord, will you fill?
I want to take back Further Still."

"Child, can't you see, I'll be here next,
The time you need to climb this crest
Changes coming, always will
Be need for reaching Further Still."

Time So Swift

Sweet bloom of youth, so quick to fade.
Left now with the choices made.
Now walking out the plan we've laid,
As time so swiftly flies.

Tomorrow's turn to yesterdays,
Grand moments, now, forgotten plays,
Once new, now old familiar ways,
As time so swiftly flies.

Years and months so brief condense,
Days long gone, sure makes no sense,
Future plans, quickly past tense,
As time so swiftly flies

So much to do, each moment full,
Ardent passions ebb then cool.
Left now, lasting love, to fuel,
As time so swiftly flies.

Little hands, now big as mine,
Cradles, strollers, I can't find,
Disastrous rooms mess with my mind,
As time so swiftly flies.

Some opportunities now gone,
Must place hope in the seeds we've sown.
From little boy, a man has grown,
As time so swiftly flies.

POURED OUT

I look into a well lined face.
An elder came, took younger place,
The girl is gone, so little trace,
As time so swiftly flies.

Have I truly done my best?
Will work of hands true stand the test?
Does satisfaction fill my breast?
As time so swiftly flies?

No other life on earth, I'm sure.
Is intent holy, motive pure?
Will I, trials well, with joy endure?
As time so swiftly flies.

ONLY YESTERDAY

It seems like only yesterday,
mottled red face pinched,
Flailing tiny fists upraised,
into this world you inched.
Like purest cotton sprang
unruly curls on perfect head,
Close examination confirmed what mom thought,
it was red!

I thought surely the heavens
would quickly miss this one so rare.
I looked into your little face
and worried, "Oh, Do I dare?"
I kissed your fuzzy cheek,
the softest down my lips would meet.
New life's aroma filled my senses,
sweet calm, so replete.

I peeled back pastel blankets
to reveal ten perfect toes.
I searched angelic features,
saw a handsome button nose.
Puckered lips, brow furled in frown,
sublime picture you did make.
I thought, Oh Lord, My hearts so full.
It's more than I can take.

You stretched and compact body became,
Oh, I'd say, inches long.
Five fingers curled round one of mine
and squeezed… He thinks he's strong.
The first night you lay in my arms,
I knew what joy true was…
Fair bald head, sweet cheeks so red,
and neck of downy fuzz.

Love, years have flown, you're almost grown,
this mother's heart is torn.
No more fair head. Feet hang off the bed.
A man these years have borne.
When I pass you in the hallway,
I often fight the urge,
To scoot to side, let you pass by,
and say excuse me, sir.

I often think to myself,
how can I bear to see him leave?
I find my heart in my throat,
hand soon tugging on your sleeve.
"Mama needs a hug, "I say.
You fold me close, so near.
I think, Oh Lord, I love him so.
Why can't he just stay here!

No woman will be good enough,
for my son, don't you know.
I squeeze a little harder,
'til strained voice says, "Mom, let go."

Precious few the years we have
to protect beneath our roof,
To kiss skinned knees, to pull from trees,
to hear the lispy tooth.

Memories, each day are made
be them great or fair.
Of late, I find myself at bedside,
thanking God you're there.
So hard to think of babes in arms,
holding babies of there own.
It comes so fast, the future past,
my little boy's full grown.

Forgive me for mistakes I've made,
while learning as I went.
For ballgames missed, boo-boo's not kissed
and special time not spent.
If I could do it over,
I know just what I would do
I'd never waste a moment
of the time I had with you.

Each time I got the chance
to sit and talk to you, I would.
I would make less of mistakes you'd made,
and emphasize the good.
I would tell you each and every day,
how blessed you make me feel.
I would spend the time with you each night,
beside the bed to kneel.

I would sing to you each morning,
a song your day to start.
I would hold you on my lap and pray,
I'd share complete my heart.
Still, there's no returning
to beginnings we've begun,
Still, we can pray, that God will make
the best of what we've done.

That is where I am, my son.
I have placed in you, my best.
But when times get tough, and you feel like giving up,
As you face another test,
Turn to the one who knows much more
than I could ever teach.
He loves you more than life itself,
and He has a grander reach.

He loaned you to me for a time,
but His you truly are.
Like oceans wild and skies of blue,
and brightest shooting star.
A purpose you were placed here for,
seek Him to find your course.
Needs you have, that man can't meet.
He alone will be your source.

Trust Him, Son, He's faithful.
He will never let you go.
Love Him, Son, He's worthy.
In wisdom you will grow.

Take Him to your bosom.
Place His words upon your head.
Talk with Him in wee hours
when you're lying in your bed.

Laugh with Him, Rejoice in Him.
Make Him your Father true.
For there will never be a parent
who can love as He loves you.
I'm thankful for my time with you.
My days will empty be.
When baby boy, his mother's joy,
leaves hearth and home and knee.

I'm always here, sweet baby dear.
My arms will always hold,
Though tall you be, at six foot three,
a son is never too old,
To crawl into his mothers lap,
and sit for moments rare,
Recalling sweet, perfect tiny feet,
and downy cotton hair.

I love you, my Sweet One!
You are a precious gift from God!

Angels & Ice Cream

*K*aitlen has always been a dreamer.

At the age of three she walked into the living room in the wee hours of the morning looking like the cherub that she was. Blonde curls in beautiful disarray, blue eyes still shadowed by sleep, she crawled into my husband's arms and curled in close. The rest... well, you can read for yourself.

ANGELS AND ICE CREAM

Awakening from nights soft arms,
Climbing clumsily from bed,
Rubbing eyes still laced with sleep,
Mussed hair standing on her head,
My little one arose this morn',
Walked straight into daddy's hug,
He pulled her close, kissed her cheek,
Held her warm and snug.
"Did you sleep well, my little one?,"
Her golden head did nod.
My heart did swell with love for her.
Oh, thank You, Father God.
Her daddy whispered in tiny ear,
"What did my baby dream?"
She smiled and looked into his eyes,
"Of Angels and Ice Cream!"
Angels and Ice cream, I sighed,
How beautiful, how dear.
Even in her dreams you show,
Your heart so purely clear.
Angels to protect her,
Ice Cream just for pleasure,
You show your hands to ever hold,
Both needs and desired treasure.
Not only do you provide
What we need to see us through,
Your greatest joy is to show Your love
In smallest hearts desire too.
So, Thank You, Lord for being there,
For instilling in all a dream,
So, we too can speak in gratitude,
Of Angels and Ice cream.

Sunset

*M*y friend, Mary, is beautiful… both inside and out. She is everything you think a woman should be. Petite, olive skin, dark hair and eyes; she is quite lovely. I probably could have handled the beauty if she were not so sweet, gentle, compassionate, merciful and genuinely anointed.

Anyway, for some reason God chose to link our hearts and our paths for a season, and I found myself constantly comparing myself to her. I wanted to look like her, speak like her, and even minister like her.

I remember quite vividly the day when the Lord pointed out the vast difference between us. We were both ministering at a women's gathering when a woman approached me concerning some family issues. Her son, a habitual wife abuser had been placed in jail for some other offense. I looked at her and said, "Good. This may be just what he needs to straighten his life out." I meant it. I truly thought it was good that he was in jail and could think about his actions.

I watched as later in the evening the same woman approached my friend, and I knew she was telling her the exact story. To my dismay, Mary threw her arms around the woman and said, "Oh, I am so sorry you are going through this…"

In that moment, I knew we were quite different… physically, fundamentally and definitely in spiritual inclination. Her driving anointing was mercy; mine was and still is prophetic. She is compassionate. I see things black and white for the most part.

Do I think I was wrong? No. Do I think Mary was wrong? No. Do I think people like her approach better than my own? Oh, definitely. Am I okay with that?

Finally.

I have now come to understand and appreciate the fact that God paints in varied colors… and oh, what a Master He is.

Sunset

Why do you spend your life admiring
someone else's sunset?
You think it is so very beautiful,
You behold the pastel colors and sigh with envy.

"Why must I walk under these clouds?" you ask.
"Why do you love her so much
more than I?
Why did you make her thus?"

He answers:

You are childish in so many ways.
If I placed upon your brow the most beautiful countenance,
Were I to hold a mirror in front of your face,
You would still see a tainted visage...
For you do not see with My eyes.
You see what others have taught you to see.

You wish and pray and hope for
what you already have.
You cry for beauty
when you posses it in plenty.
You weep for losses
that you yourself have cast away.

You believe lies
when I shout the truth from the housetop.
Prophecy given says you were painted in bold colors.
You hide
behind the brown and wheat.

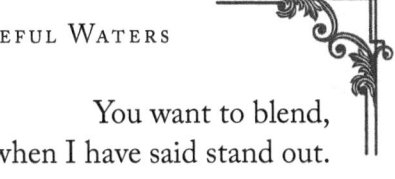

You want to blend,
when I have said stand out.

Her sunset would never satisfy you
with its pale hues.
Though peaceful and quite serene.

Look well to your own sky.
I Am the lifter of your head.

When I lift your head,
no soul can cause it to drop again in shame.
When I lift your head,
you will see your sunset.
Reds, blue, purples, gold's,
Flashes of fiery beauty,
Blazing across a canvass
prepared for you
and you alone.

Look up, Daughter!

The Master is painting!"

A Gift of Service

We are His hands extended. We are His hands withheld. We make the choice. The decision is ours, as is the fruit of that decision, be it good or bad.

My mother, a minister and pastor of her own flock, has, for many years led a thriving nursing home ministry. Every Tuesday morning for the last fifteen years, barring illness or unforeseen circumstance, Mama has shown up on the doorstop of the tiny nursing home just down the road from her little farmhouse. Well worn Bible in hand, song in heart, she eagerly makes the rounds, room to room, bringing the crippled, tired, wheelchair bound, mentally challenged, Alzheimer gripped, needy, aging saints of God, into the small meeting room, to share with them the great hope of the gospel of Jesus Christ. Rain or shine, she is there. She loves God's own in His stead. Her faithful ministry has brought comfort to the dying, solace to the grieving, help to the helpless... His hands extended.

Therefore, I was somewhat surprised one morning while visiting with her, when she made a request of me. She wanted me to write a poem for all of the wonderful people who worked at the nursing home. It was her intent to honor them for all of the hours of hard work and dedication. She wanted them to know that their years of service did not go unnoticed and that they were appreciated. I smiled as she made this request, and told her that, of course, I would pray about it and ask God to give me something specifically for them.

I was struck by the great irony of the request, for the poem she asked of me would also be in honor of her. She, of course, could never see it, for in the midst of her service to the Master, all she could see was the labor of the others in the field. She failed to recognize that in order to see the labor of others so closely, she too, must have been toiling alongside.

The following poem is one of specificity, but lends itself ever so gently to the general service of the saints of God.

For we are all His hands extended...or withheld.

A GIFT OF SERVICE
(His hands extended...)

Many have forgotten
these ones you gently hold,
So oft alone, life's service done,
family hearts grown cold.
You take them to your bosom,
love them in My stead,
See that they are warm and safe,
bathed and loved and fed.

The greatest of commands is met,
though your life seem on the shelf,
You've taken these, My aging saints,
and loved them as yourself.
Whenever they do cry out,
their memories gripping tight,
Take their hands and stroke their hair,
speak peace to troubled night.

Years of lonely labor,
you have spent upon this task,
Great is your reward, My child,
and you have but to ask.
As you have met the needs of these,
so I yours, will quickly meet,
Call on Me when strength fades swift,
find solace at My feet.

As you extend the gentle hand
and stroke a well lined face,
So will I be quick to soothe your pain
with strokes of grace.

When sorrow wracks your body,
for loss of those so dear,
Brief speak My name, sweet comfort find,
for I am ever near.

I share your joyous laughter,
I feel your grief My own,
I bottle up the tears you shed,
precious seeds that you have sown.
I'm forever in the middle
of the labor of your hands,
I know how hard it is some days
to meet such great demands.

Oh, how beautifully you have managed,
report of you is great,
For I speak with those you have comforted,
When I meet them at My gate.

They speak ever so fondly
of kindness' you have dealt.
They tell Me of your gentleness,
and of tenderness they felt,
When in their final days on earth,
you sheltered them from harm,
Delivering them quite safely
to the Father's waiting arms.

Your service is one without price.

Teacher

Do you know we love you?
Do you know just what you've done?
Do you recognize the lives you've changed?
The healings you've begun?

Can you see the fruit of labor dear?
Can you sense His mighty hand,
In placing you before our eyes,
Sister, do you understand?

What you have wrought these years of past,
Your service plain to see,
Will not be full, completely known,
'Til wrapped in love's eternity.

One day beside you we will stand,
And tell our Master True,
Of our precious teachers heart,
Of her words that helped us through.

We will tell Him how you cared for us,
How you led us to His feet,
Then taught us quick to take our failures,
To His Mercy Seat.

You know we need not tell Him all,
For all He's watched through time.
I see Him looking down on you and smiling,
"Yes, She's mine."

He takes the greatest pleasure,
In watching over you.
He loves the way your heart responds,
'What would my Savior have me do?'

Compassion from His throne does flow,
Through your gentle hand.
We've oft been the recipient,
'Twas His awesome perfect plan.

Your life has changed the course of ours,
Your teaching fills us so,
We take this moment just to say...
We love you more than you can know!

Precious Father,
Thank You for my Teacher.

THE COVERING

Say what you will about me,
Feel free to scorn this name.
Make fun of what I do or say
To me it is all the same.

Still, mark these words,
Heed well this charge,
My warning be not mild,
You stir a mighty hornet's nest,
When your barbs do strike my child.

A mighty lion does soon ignore,
The pesky taunting beast,
But if the torments touch its young,
It is soon the Lion's feast.

So it is, with my Father dear,
There's much that He will take,
But harm one hair on His child's fair head,
Watch mountains start to quake.

The millstone hung around the neck,
Was not promised for His shame,
But vengeance wrought to those who hurt,
Small ones who bore His name.

Selah

Pause calmly and think upon these things!

Daddy, I Remember

I had some issues with my Father.
I can look at that sentence and smile now.
I could not look at it and smile when it said *have* instead of *had*.
He left when I was 10.
He kept leaving—in my mind—until I was in my 20s.
Some things you get over.
Some things you say you get over.
I said a lot.
It took longer to do.
Today, I am 40 and I am healed…
my issues no longer issues.
I share with you from the old pages…

Did you know… I look like my Father?

Daddy, I remember...

I remember the way you smelled,
like Old Spice and hard work.

I remember the sound of your voice
when you laughed
like dry sunshine,
all raspy and warm.
Your eyes had tiny crinkles in the corners
from laughing hard and often.

I remember the feel of your hand
as it held mine,
square, strong, callused
and safe...

I remember the way the grass smelled...
after you mowed it...
wearing Bermuda shorts...
and black dress boots.

I remember the way you looked at mama,
right before you snuck up behind her in the kitchen,
wrapped your arms around her...
and made her smile a secret smile.

I remember the way you played the guitar,
while all of us girls laughed and danced around your feet.
I remember the first time I sang with you in church,
"...born again, free from sin, I'm happy night and day..."

Daddy, I remember...

Missing you after you'd gone...
Watching for you...
Listening for the sound of your car...

Not caring if you came...

Caring...
Not understanding... Understanding...

Hurting... Praying...

Forgiving... Not forgetting...
Forgiving again...

Now, I remember...

All of the good things.
The wonderful, loving, man that you were.
The lives you touched and changed.
The souls that were won to my Savior because of you.

The way that you smelled,
Of Old Spice and hard work.

Daddy, I remember...

And I miss you...

Daddy Look at Me
a child's song of lament

She seemed so small and lonely,
When she walked into the room.
She had this distant haunted look.
Her pretty dress twirled round her feet,
As she gently swayed.
She hummed her secret tune.
Patent leather's quietly shuffled,
She waited patiently.

Daddy look at me,
I'm so glad you finally came,
I wore this dress just for you.
Would you dance with me?
Would you hold my hand?
Will you spin me round and round,
'Til I'm dizzy and can't breathe?
Daddy look at me,
I'm trying so hard to be,
The best girl in the world,
Oh, please daddy!

He grabbed his suitcase, crossed the floor
Barely saw her there...
He had that distant haunted look.
A silent tear slid down her cheek,
She quietly turned away.
She felt the slamming of the door.
Patent leathers quietly shuffled,
As she wiped the tears away...

Her words, they echoed,
Daddy, look at me...

Excuses

"Oh, my goodness!" I cried.
"No, My goodness!" He replied.

"I need to do..."
"I've already done!"

"But, Lord, I think..."
"My thoughts are higher than your thoughts..."

"Lord, I'm worried..."
"Will that add one inch to your height, one hour to your life?"

"Oh, I'm scared...!"
"I did not give you this spirit of fear..."

"Lord, the people caused..."
"Look well to your own personality..."

"I just get so angry..."
"Sin not in your anger..."

"You just don't understand..."
"For you have a high priest who is touched
by the very feelings of your infirmities..."

"But, I get so tired, Lord..."
"If you wait on Me, I will renew your strength..."

"Well, if they treat me like this, I'll just..."
"If it depends on your actions, live at peace with everyone..."

"It's my duty to tell them what I think..."
"It is a wise man who guards his tongue..."

"God made me this way, I'm can't help it if I sin..."
"Let no man say that I have brought temptation to him..."

"Well, I think they have a real problem..."
"With the measure you use to judge, will you be judged..."

"Lord, I really don't understand..."
"Lean on My understanding, child..."

"I'm just high-strung..."
"Let My peace mount guard over your hearts and minds..."

"It's just too hard..."
"With Me, all things are possible..."

"God, they don't like me, they ridicule me..."
"Count it all joy!"

"I really want to quit..."
"Do not weary of doing well, for in due season you will reap..."

"He hurts my feelings..."
"Trust Me..."

"I feel alone in this..."
"Never will I leave you or forsake you..."

"But, I'm not anybody special..."
"You are the righteousness of God in Christ..."

"I'm very weak, Lord..."
"What a wonderful opportunity for Me to be strong for you..."

"I feel so far away from You..."
"Neither height nor depth....will separate My love from you..."

"I need You every minute of every day, Lord..."
"Yes, I know. That's why I came!"

EXPOSED

I'm feeling exposed and vulnerable.
I just shared my frailties, okay, my hidden sins, with a sister.
She felt like she had failed me,
I felt my "standing" in her eyes slip.
I tried to close my mouth,
The confession seemed to roll from lips refusing restraint.
She looked hurt and surprised,
I thought I must look quite weak and foolish.
I thought I had just placed a big pink elephant in the room,
God love her,
She thought the elephant was a mouse.
Perception is funny that way.
To eyes distorted by fear and shame,
A mouse might take on the appearance of an elephant.
Lord, I really feel exposed.
I really do not like this feeling, I whined.
"You will become well acquainted with this feeling.
After all, what do you think "poured out" means?" He answered.

The Flesh

I find no freedom from this fear,
To begin and then not stop.
Pushing fuel, way beyond full,
Running over the top.

I hate it, Lord! I hate it so!
Why do I do such things?
I hurt so bad, I do not stop,
When I know the pain it brings.

I tell myself it's just this once.
Tomorrow I'll start new,
But trust is lost, so great the cost,
Unfaithful now to You.

It truly isn't worth it, Lord.
I hate the food I crave.
But somehow I bow to its side,
Fools court an early grave.

So sick, the feeling I now have,
Compulsion ruled in place,
Of faithful loving Father's hand,
And gentle Saviors face.

Help me, Lord! I loath myself.
I hate what I've become,
So slow of foot, so large in girth,
There's nowhere left to run!

Oh, rescue me again, my love,
Call my name once more.
Release me from these prison bonds,
My heart to 'Thee will soar.

Make me new, fair Master dear,
Do not trust me to my hand.
No wisdom in the paths I choose,
I fail to understand.

As Paul, so oft I find myself,
Doing what I'd wish not do.
Sin's nature cries aloud through flesh
Submitted not to You.

So, here I am King, once again,
A servant to this base.
I fall to knees, sweet Father please,
Teach me to seek Your face.

Rescue me, my heart is sore,
From beatings born within,
Heal fresh this child, give me Your strength,
To rise, begin again.

I place my hope in you alone, Father!

Dirt Roads

I grew up in a small town in east Tennessee. The beautiful rolling hills lay just outside the dusty curtains that hang haphazardly above my bedroom window. In the mornings, I was awakened by the sound of birds singing, the mournful moan of our red-bone hound dog, Bum, and the sound of my mother bangin' pots in the kitchen as she scrambled eggs and fried sausage. I could tell exactly when it was time to get up, 'cause I'd smell the biscuits browning.

My summer days consisted of fighting with my younger sister, Angie, then playing games with her. We knew those hills like our own backyard, for that is just what they were. We played *Lost in Space*—she always got to be Judy because of her blonde hair-, hide and seek, freeze tag, bicycle races, stomped through muddy creek beds, caught butterflies, lightening bugs, frogs, crawfish. We simply enjoyed life. A simple life. We lacked for nothing and wanted everything. I remember laughing loud and often. I remember jokes, smiles, music. I remember the way my father smelled on Sunday morning before church. I remember how beautiful my mom looked in her red suit.

I remember so many things; still others are reduced to images, feelings, smells. They are triggered by the strangest things. Going on a field trip with my son, sitting on his bus, I was carried back to another bus, thirty years before. The seats stuck to my legs in the same way. The bus driver peered through the overhead mirror in the same manner; you know that kind of searching-scowl that all bus drivers develop over time. I was suddenly six years old, on my way to school. I felt the same little rush, the empty feeling in the pit of my stomach. I shook my head to clear the deja-vu webs.

I lived in a butterscotch-colored house on a dirt road called Walls Hollow. My dad built the house after our trailer burned down one night while we were at the stock car races. Does that sound redneck enough for you? I loved our butterscotch house. I never asked why daddy painted it that color, but looking back, I feel reasonably certain that the paint must have been a good deal. Back then, I just thought it was beautiful. I felt calm when I looked at that house. I felt safe living in that house.

When my grandpa was pouring our concrete sidewalk he let all of us girls, four at that time, put our hands in the wet cement. Four perfect little handprints sealed in time. It was fun then, it makes me cry now.

A year or so ago I went back to the old house. The new owners had changed everything. The house had been enlarged, outbuild-ings added. My old basketball goal was now home to a couple of cars. The garden my daddy had planted every year was gone, the yard swing absent, as well. A couple of things remained, however. Wonderful things that called me back again, to a time that now exists only in my mind.

Sitting beside the kitchen door was the dogwood tree I had loved as a child. In the springtime, it had large white blooms with crimson edges. My mother had stood with me at that dogwood tree and shared the story of how the bloom represented the cross of Christ. I remember how tenderly she held the flower as she explained its legend. I remember her hands. I look at my own hands now to see hers. They are the same.

As I approached the walk, I was almost afraid to look. Thirty years had come and gone since papaw had knelt with us, pressing chubby fingers into wet, gritty cement. What if they had erased the handprints? Would proof of my childhood also be erased? I wanted so badly to see the four tangible imprints of my lost youth. I walked slowly, eyes shut tight as I approached the place where they had once been. I took a deep breath, counted to three, tilted my head forward and opened my eyes. They were there! I exhaled. Just as they had been thirty years earlier. Their imprint more shallow, yet undeniably there.

I knelt beside what I felt almost an effigy of the little girl I had been. My now wrinkled, dishpan hand, trembled as it cautiously traced the edges of a much smaller one. I looked at my sisters hands beside my own and flashes of a lifetime skittered through my mind. Tears, unchecked, spilled from my eyes as I mourned the loss of those tender, innocent years, then those tears were replaced by tears of triumph as I realized that all four of these little hands still led full, blessed lives. Not one of those children had been lost over the years. They all still loved one another, still played 'house' together—only for real this time, still spent holidays together, still rambled through the unchanging, beautiful hills of East Tennessee...

They all still laughed ...

loud and often...

Dirt Roads

There's a house of butterscotch
Slumbering just down the road
Often times I travel there
Just to let my mind unfold.
I sit beneath the dogwood tree,
Touch the handprints on the walk,
If I listen close enough,
I can hear the old walls talk...

Here comes the wind, The leaves they turn.
The pictures change, Still I have learned,
That all I've known, Still walks with me,
Down the dirt roads.

Daddy's mowing in the yard
Wearing high top leather boots,
Little girls play upon the swing,
In their faded summer suits.
Sweet Mama in the kitchen there,
She's never hard to find.
My sweet constant companions
On the back roads of my mind.

Come on wind...

Years pass swift and little girls
Hold babies of their own,
They leave the house of butterscotch,
Still, they're forever comin' home...

POURED OUT

So, come on wind, leaves that turn,
The pictures change, but I have learned,
All I know will walk with me,
Down these dirt roads.

Important or Impotent

Musings from a mother's heart...

*T*o get the full effect of the following, you must imagine a squeaky, high-pitched three-year-old voice singing with all its might! Words mispronounced, running together...you know, the most beautiful sound on earth.)

> *Pieces passes understandin,*
> *Down in my heart.*
> *Where?! (shouted!!!)*
> *Down in my heart.*
> *Where!?*
> *Down in my heart.*
> *Where...*
> (You get the picture)
> *And I am happy, I'm very happy..."*

Such a tiny little body;
Such tiny little three-year-old hands;
Such a great big voice!
Such a pounding headache, as those same tiny hands pound out an indecipherable tune on a big, old, noisy piano right next to the computer where I now sit.
Such a wonderful problem to have!

Doesn't she see that mommy is doing important things?

As I was writing the previous sentence, I accidentally left the "r" out of important, revealing the true meaning behind what I am attempting to say upon this page. Yes, I know impotent is spelled with an "e" and not an "a" but you get the overall gist, right? I am talking about the things we spend our time on that really will not matter in the grand finale of life. The "works" that will be burned up before the Lord. What do we set our hand to? To what do we apply our strength? To whom do we give devotion? From whom do we withhold devotion?

Questions to ponder before the Mercy Seat and at the Throne of Grace. For, truly, upon self-examination, I find myself seeking the mercy and grace of My God who searches heart, intent, and reveals to me the real reasons...

Why do I do the things I do?

Important or Impotent

Important is the feeling you get when your child looks into your eyes and truly believes your kiss is going to magically heal her skinned knee.
Impotent is what you are when you cannot take time to kiss the knee.

Important is the time spent reading to your child at bed-time, praying with them then holding them in your arms as they fall asleep.
Impotent is yelling across the room, "say your prayers," then never taking their little hand and showing them how.

Important is taking your child to church and showing great pleasure at being in the house of the Lord.
Impotent is dropping them off at the front door of the church while you go do your errands, or take it easy for a while.

Important is quantity time. For "quality time" cannot be truly appreciated by a three year old who just wants to be with Mommy and Daddy.

Important is everything we say, but even more so, what we do.
Impotent is never doing what we say.

A child knows the difference!

Barely Hangin' On

Walk on by, walk on by,
Forget me on this ledge so high,
Desperation, sound your sigh,
I'm barely hangin' on.

Hands are bleeding, wrists are sore,
I try to hold a little more,
Fingertips slide 'cross the floor,
I'm barely hangin on.

Crying once, calling twice,
Who will pay this torments price?
None but one sure will suffice,
I'm barely hangin' on.

Must be blind, don't see me here,
Footsteps sound, so many near,
My hands are trampled, cries they cant hear,
I'm barely hangin' on.

Desperate now, can't do a thing,
Come gentle wind of mighty wings,
Lovers' voice so sweetly sings,
She's barely hangin' on.

Swiftly! Swiftly! Bring to Me,
My small ones falling, can't you see?
I'll hold her close now. My child can't be,
Barely hangin' on.

I See You

My wonderful friend has nine children. I know, it almost takes your breath away. I mean, we feel like our world is turned upside-down when only one appears on the scene. Nevertheless, what I have found is that once you are upside-down it truly does not matter how many enter the scene.

Christine is a wonderful mother. With children ranging in age from 26 to 3, all healthy, bright and well mannered, I can truly say, the woman has outdone herself. I sometimes stand in awe as I watch her love and hug and feed and dress and discipline this beautiful brood. How blessed she and her husband are. If I have ever witnessed a woman walking in her destiny it has most definitely been Christine. She amazes me.

Still, there was one particular day when I could see the weariness in her stride. I know it should not have surprised me, but it somehow captured my thoughts. I stood back and looked at her with different eyes, and believe I caught a glimpse of Jesus' heart toward her. I sat and penned this poem as thoughts of her extraordinarily eternal mission on this planet permanently penetrated this temporal mind.

I See You

I see you, little mother.
Yes, you, with wringing hand.
My heart is touched by cries of yours,
and yes, I understand.
"So much to do, so little time."
I've said those words myself.
"This days too long, still much undone.
My life upon the shelf."

I looked for those to help me,
yet, the brunt was mine alone.
You think you'll wither on the vine,
then turn to find you've grown.
So soon it will be over,
the trouble, trial and tears,
But with it, children's laughter.
You'll miss it in those years.

At times, I thought my load too much,
too heavy, just as you.
I fell to knees, with heart poured out,
"Daddy, help me, too!"
He came and brought me comfort,
just as I do send you now,
With gentle words, encouragement.
Keep hand set to that plow.

The fruit of labor far from seen,
yet, planted midst your toil,
A wealth of seed to harvest.
Well tilled, your verdant soil.

Great price is paid for precious things,
My life has borne this true.
Invest, my little mother.
Reward comes swift to you.

At times when you feel all alone,
know that I felt the same,
When backs were turned, hands withheld,
and hatred rode my name.
Yet, just as I, your time will come.
Walk patiently, with hope.
You see the smaller picture here,
but I've the grander scope.

Like waters sent throughout the earth,
your little ones will bring,
To heart's in Satan's winter,
Christ's sweet breath of spring.
So, when it all seems endless,
Take courage. You be strong.
For the prayers of little mother's
are ere before My throne...

Yes, I See You!

Last Sunday

I sat by you last Sunday.
I sang the songs, knew all of the words.
I smiled when appropriate, forced a laugh when necessary.
At one point, the minister encouraged us to greet one another.
Yes! I thought. She'll notice me now.
Surely, she'll see beyond this "church face."
You didn't.
You shook hands with one person. One person that you knew.

I sat by you last Sunday.
I cried through the entire service.
You could not see.
The tears ran down my soul, not my face.
Did you know that all week I have despaired of life?
Do you care that I am overwhelmed?
Just one word and I would have crumbled into your arms.

I sat by you last Sunday.
Before I took my seat, I prayed, "God please help me."
All of a sudden, there you were sitting down beside me.
I knew your reputation.
Sunday School Teacher, Women's Ministry.
You knew how to touch the heart of God!
Hope rose quickly within me!
"Oh, thank you God. You have heard my prayer."
You barely glanced my way.

I sat by you last Sunday.
I did not want you to be God to me,
Just show me His love.
I did not need you to perform a miracle,

just care enough to pray for one.
I did not need you to be a perfect minister,
just my sister.

I sat by you last Sunday.
Do you know that I am bound tightly by drugs?
Can you see beyond the dress and the make-up?
Can you guess that Satan torments me with my past to the
point that I literally lose my breath?
Do you care that I am bowing to bulimia?
What do you see when you look at me?
Have you ever really looked?

I sat by you last Sunday.
I left feeling worse than when I had entered.
I know you are not my God;
I did not look to you for healing.
You are my sister;
I looked to you for compassion,
gentle human touch.
His kindness distributed through your hands.

I sat by you last Sunday.
Do you remember me?
Would you recognize me if I sat by you again?
Will you remember my words?
Will you seek me out?
Will you continue look inward, or will you reach out?
Will you encourage me with His precious word from your own lips?

Oh please....
Look for me.
I'm easy to find...
I sat by you last Sunday.

MARY'S CALL

Let the laundry sit awhile,
I've something better planned.
It's time to take a journey,
To a fairer promised land.

Let me show you all the things,
Your eyes yet do not see.
Follow close, heed sure this voice,
Come travel child, with Me.

Vistas before now unseen,
Revealed before your eyes,
Rolling Mountains, windswept lakes,
Souring, peaceful skies.

This is where your spirit runs,
When solace it does seek,
Find it here, your Passion near,
Lovers' words I'll speak.

I oft meet with my children here,
It takes no time at all,
To find this place, quick, seek My face,
Then gently to knee fall.

I call so often to you child,
My voice you fail to hear,
For radios, and cares and woes,
TVs, plans and fear.

So, I will call you to a quiet place,
Still, you must make the choice,
To come and see, leave all for Me,
Come listen to My voice.

We will journey to a land prepared,
A calling you need meet,
'Tis not too far, for 'ere you are,
It is found easily at My Feet.

This is where I show you all,
Gain vision small or grand,
This is where you learn to seek,
My face and not My Hand.

Not a lowly place, dear one,
So high this call to grace,
Never more exalted than the time
Spent on your face.

Here at My feet, this journey take,
This place is yours alone.
Precious oil from heart does flow,
When broken at My Throne.

What lies within will soon be known,
There is nothing hidden here.
For a heart laid bare, its secrets shown,
Will have no cause to fear.

The hidden cannot harm you,
When freely taken to the light,
It's what we keep inside,
That lends itself to sleepless night.

Freedom in this land is yours,
You have but to claim,
Let deed be done, sweet victory won,
You will never be the same.

Your captivity led captive,
Let incense so replete,
Cry to all who venture near,
Come sit at the Master's feet!"

"For Mary has chosen the better thing..."

I Need You

Will you hold me when other arms are closed?
Will you speak kind words of love...
when my heart aches from bruises inflicted by harshness?
Will you look at me and see beauty...
when other eyes fail to see anything remotely pretty?
Oh Father, I need You so....

Will your eyes smile in pleasure when they glance my way?
Will you overlook the small failures...
when others seem to hold them under a magnifying glass?
Will your gentle rain of compassion cover...
me when others sit down to judge?
Oh Father, I need You so....

Will You talk with me when others have no time?
Will you listen to and take pleasure in my songs and poetry?
Will You understand what I feel when I write?
Will You hold me...
when the tears will not cease no matter what I do?
Oh Father, I need You so...

Will You find my thoughts provoking,
my conversation stimulating...
when others wear a mask of boredom?
Will You hide me away...
When I am hurting so bad that I cannot face the world for this day?
Will You be my best friend and companion...
when I am utterly alone?
Oh Father, I need You so...

POURED OUT

Will You be everything to me?
Will You fill the gaping holes in this heart?
Will You exchange my wickedness for Your goodness?

Oh Father, I need You so...

A Cry For Recompense

Their anger goes before them, Lord.
Their tongues breathe fire and wrath.
No running from them, this is sure,
    They are directly in my path.

They hate the truth, lies are their choice,
    They would snare me on my way.
My flesh does rise, frustration cries,
    "Each word to them repay!"

Is it unfitting to want to right,
    Wrongs unjustly dealt?
Does my heart lay pure before You,
    When I feel the things I've felt?

A part of me wants to lie down,
    Pretend be lost in dream,
The other part, the cry of heart,
    Feels like it wants to scream.

I am tired, Lord. My strength is weak,
    Must force my feet to task,
I need you Lord, the truth to speak,
    It is recompense, I ask.

Quiet the tongues that rise to judge,
    Rebuke evil hearts intent,
Remove the pain of malicious words,
    Restore tears I have spent.

You are my King, You are in control,
Please make Your presence known.
Shut lions mouth, from north to south,
Deceitful hearts will groan.

Forgive me for not trusting You,
Making my plans, not Your own.
Please help me always recognize,
My Victory is in The Throne.

I love You My Lord, My Help.
My Recompense...

The Mess

Knock, Knock upon the door...
"May I come in?" the question raised.
I peered through keyhole, instant the cry,
Not Him! it's cleaning day!

I could not just let Him stand there,
So, I opened up the door,
The foyers clean, I thought.
He can stand there, nothing more.

He stepped inside, I blocked the way.
He gave a knowing look,
He nodded toward the open room,
Yes, that was all it took.

Oh, what a mess, I cringed inside.
Now what will He think?
We've made it past the living room...
Oh, No Lord, not the sink!

You know that is my private mess,
I even covered it, you see...
He smiled that smile, as if to say,
It is not hidden from Me.

Just when I thought I'd faint from shame,
I felt His gentle hand,
I looked into His loving eyes,
And I began to understand.

I offered Him my drink of praise,
Served from chipped and faded cup,
For He hadn't come to judge the mess,
But to help me clean it up.

85

LEARNING AS I GO

Oh, Father, how I love You,
Why You love me, I don't know,
I must surely test Your patience,
For, I'm learning as I go.

I said I wouldn't do that thing,
That always bows me low,
But wayward child I am, I failed,
Still, I'm learning as I go.

One moment I can change the world,
The next tossed to and fro,
Like a boat that seeks the shore,
I'm learning as I go.

The hope that pushes me onward,
Is one day Your voice I'll know,
Then it will be much easier,
This learning as I go.

Summits rise before me,
The Spirit's wind does blow,
Leading me through pathways safe,
Learning as I go.

Too Much

"Here we go again,"
   persistent cry of double-mind
"Oh, I know, I know the answer,"
   but somehow, it's hard to find.
"I've decided now, but then again,
   maybe I'm not sure."
I set my sight only to find
   I'm drawn by subtle lure.

"You didn't really hear His voice,
   it could've been your own."
Whispered torments, questions raised,
   confusions wind is blown.
"Set your mind! Are you so weak,
   your thoughts you can't control. "
Constant reminders, taunting cries,
   such torment to my soul.

Why can't my heart for all time set
   on what I know is true?
Why can't I lift petitions,
   knowing the answer comes from You?
What have I let my mind come to?
   What seeds have deep been sown?
Childish places trod by one
   who should be quite full grown.

Can I get it back, dear Lord?
   Can I make the torment cease?
"Only when you give it all to Me,
   will you find peace.

You were not called as others;
   your call is quite unique.
You cannot serve as others serve,
   child, daily your must seek,

My face, My hand, My favor,
   My peace, My yoke, My will,
Nothing else will ever consume
   the void you try to fill.
Confusion claims its victims
   when they are least aware,
Minds occupied with foolishness,
   and eyes not set with care.

You do not guard that which I give,
   you cast aside with ease.
You look for smiling, easy words
   and lies so sure to please.
You disregard the truth you know,
   desires, they rule your walk,
You've turned your mouth to idle things,
   no faith left in your talk.

If it's the truth you're seeking here,
   not mere scratch of itching ears,
Listen close, I will give to you
   the wisdom of My years.
Oh, but wait, I've done just that.
   My word has come to you,
It's all laid out, your answers there;
   you know what you must do.

Set time aside; make Me the first thing
   that you crave each day,

My words will fill you, My love heal you,
    and send you on your way.
Your life is so much more than days
    long spent on eat and drink.
Your victory lies in everything
    you do and say and think.

So set your mind on higher things,
    seek Me always first,
Single minded you'll become,
    then I can quench your thirst.
Your ravenous in search of something,
    you're hungry for my touch,
But when I reach, you run from Me,
    crying, "Oh it's just too much!"

Too much—too hard?
    You know 'tis not true
Too much is watching a child of mine
    be beaten black and blue.
Too much is seeing My own Son
    be nailed high on a tree,
So you can turn, live life your way,
    come running back to Me!

The mess is made, now clean it up!
    The tools are in your hand.
I have heard your prayer!
    The answers there!
Now you must make a stand!"

A Poem of Assuage

Cry out, cry out, wounded soul,
Wells of pain release.
Fall, Oh fall to knee, hearts pride,
Trade folly great for peace.

Tender, tender mercies find,
Rain, sweet rain of tears.
Perfect, perfect spirit calm,
Transcending lifeless years.

Faithful, Faithful, Father He,
Children run and see.
Play, Oh play in splendid bliss,
Loose dark chains, be free!

Done, it's done! Battle be gone,
Victory's scent is sweet.
Rest, Oh rest, fair Presence found,
Tears bathe The Master's feet.

MY BELOVED

Come, Oh Come, my Bridegroom dear,
My heart does call Your name.
But one touch from Your sweet hand,
Ne're will I be the same.
Long, Oh long, this aching heart,
For One whose name is all.
Sweetest voice soon will I hear,
For He, to me will call.
Look, Oh Look, upon His face,
Fairest, lover see,
Turn your cheek into his hand,
His love does flow through thee.
Hold, Oh Hold, the strongest arms,
Rest safely troubled head.
For He has come, The Lovely One.
There's nothing more to dread.
Heart, Oh Heart, consumed by flame,
Passions fire refined.
For at last, I am Beloved's
And He is Truly Mine.

GROOM

I cannot do this anymore,
Lord, You will have to take my hand.
I haven't any strength to fight,
Father, I can barely stand.

The weight of all I'm carrying,
Has drained my joy complete,
This heart does faint within my chest,
My needs Lord, I can't meet.

I struggle and I struggle,
My tears do sorely fall,
But pride does push my feet ahead,
Too haughty now to call.

Step by step my feet do sink,
Deeper into this mire,
Still I press onward, seeking my ways,
Chasing my own desire.

Panting now, my lungs exhaust,
You are far beyond my reach.
Stumble into darkness swift,
Can You this chasm breach?

"Oh what a question, silly child,
My hand is long indeed.
There's nothing that I will not do for you,
If there be need.

You struggle because you do not ask,
Before you leap ahead.
A greater wisdom will be found,
When you seek my heart instead.

Your burdens they are great,
When on small shoulders they are borne,
But upon your My mighty Saviors arms,
The yoke is swiftly torn.

Exhausted days have ruled your life,
For joy you cannot find,
But set your eyes upon My word,
And My peace will guard your mind.

Double minded? Yes, you are,
For you do not know My will,
Single hearted you will become,
Come thirsty, drink your fill.

You say you need deliverance,
But discipline, I'd say,
Is what you need develop
In your time with Me each day.

Make a choice, My little one.
Be either cold or hot,
For heed Me, I desire your all,
But left-over is what I've got.

All I have is given to.
The Bride who's chosen to,
Give her whole heart to the Groom,
To find His love is true.

Faithful I have always been,
Faithful I will be,
To the one who follows ever.
Whole hearted after Me.

If you knew Me better,
There'd surely be no doubt,
For to cherish the Bride completely,
Is what This Bridegrooms all about."

You can entrust Me with your heart...

MORE

Help me, Lord, my heart is bruised,
I'm feeling deep down, hurting, used,
My mind is reeling, so confused,
I know there must be more.

I've walked it, talked it, played the game,
Called on You, no other name,
Still circumstances stay the same,
I know there must be more.

I'm holding heavy chains of doubt,
I lack the strength to see this out,
I question what I'm all about,
I know there must be more.

The very core of who I am,
Cries from deep, "it's a sham.'
The water rages against the dam,
I know there must be more.

I know that once I knew You well,
Great testimony have I to tell,
Can You show me where it was I fell?
I know there must be more.

On the surface, smiles do play,
Can't let them see me any other way,
Just have to make it through today,
I know there must be more.

I'm walking high upon this rope,
Searching for my missing hope,

Trying very hard to cope,
I know there must be more.

Give and give, then give some more,
Start over where I was before,
My spirit prostrate on the floor,
I know there must be more.

Filled too many times to speak,
Contents spill from soulish leak,
Always struggling, still no peak,
I know there must be more.

Lord, I turn my eyes to You,
Nowhere to run, nothing to do,
My heart is beaten black and blue,
I know there must be more.

What will it take to gain the lost?
When will I cease to count the cost?
When will you melt this fleshly frost?
I know there must be more.

Rise, Oh rise, my spirit man,
Look to heaven while you can,
Living water for thirsty land,
I know there must be more.

Hold me to Your heart my King,
Take this offering I bring,
A song of brokenness I sing,
I know there must be more.

Adonai, Adonai, Adonai

Complete Me

There are times when I feel like I am never going to get there. The fickleness of this flesh that I dwell in astounds even me at times. One day I am on top of the world, can accomplish anything, spend hours in the Word and pray all day long. The very next morning I may just wake up with a "woe-is-me" attitude and not want to face the world. I am learning as I go.

I know that My Father is working even in the foolishness of my ways. He is trying to let me know that it does not matter how I feel in my physical body, I have a choice to make as to how my day is going to proceed from moment to moment. Do I give in to the bad mood, or do I make the decision to have another kind of day? I believe with all of my heart, that I set myself up with the words of my mouth and the thoughts that I allow to run unchecked through this mind of mine. I can make or break my own day with a simple decision. No, not name-it-claim-it. I mean a positive outlook on a life controlled by Someone who loves you more than life itself.

I find myself relating all too well to Paul's writings in Romans. The things I do not want to do, are the things that I find myself doing. The things that I want to do, I do not do. Yuck! I really dislike this part of me. I want to be the me that God wants me to be, but I somehow find myself often taking the easy road, which leads to a mediocre me. I know He has so much more planned for this life I am living. I keep reminding myself that He is faithful to complete what He started. He knew what He was getting when He called me. I am no surprise to God. He knows how to deal with me, and I trust Him to complete me...

COMPLETE ME

No need to wallow in despair,
Mere lift of eyes will find you there,
Free to lay aside this care,
I know You will complete me.

Many failures, small and great,
Often found on knee of late,
Pounding soundly on the gate,
I know You will complete me.

Sometimes I want to run away,
Soon, come Your voice to bid me stay,
From hiding place to full light day,
I know You will complete me.

Much left to do, Sweet Lord, I know,
My feet stand firm when You cry "Go".
Disobedience bows me low,
I know You will complete me.

Seems a long way home to You,
Get lost in things I should not do,
Come running back to Lover True,
I know You will complete me.

Ups and downs do mark my course,
Drawn aside by unseen force,
Heart bruised sore with great remorse,
I know You will complete me.

At times all hope away does fade,
Erased by vast mistakes I've made,
Crumpled paper plans I've laid,
I know You will complete me.

A work in progress, this I'm sure,
Still wooed by the Father's lure,
One day motives will be pure,
I know You will complete me.

Rawest clay to meet Your hand,
You alone Lord, understand,
What form to shape this life You've planned,
I know You will complete me.

Great confidence I have in You,
I've witnessed what grand work you do,
Paint boldest color, brightest hue,
I know You will complete me.

Two works never be the same,
Linked firmly by a Fathers name,
To halt such process would cry shame,
I know You will complete me.

Paint me, mold me, twist the clay,
Canvas awaits the Master's play,
Ever looking to the day,
I know You will complete me.

Nothing to Offer

Do you ever have times when you just cannot figure out for the life of you what it was that God thought He was getting when He chose you? Do you ever wonder if He regrets His choice? I probably should not admit to such thoughts, but I cannot help but wonder if there are others out there, who, like me, know beyond a shadow of a doubt that they got the good end of the deal in this exchange with God. Today's society scorns such a deal as the typical, "If it sounds too good to be true..."

Ah, but it is that good and it is most definitely true.

Maybe that is why we struggle so hard with the idea that we can do absolutely nothing to make things come out even. We push and push, and perform and perform; attempting to be good enough to receive what He has already freely given to us. It is so 'human' to think we will ever be good enough to earn this gift of God.

I am awed by the simplicity of salvation. It is so elementary it confounds the wise men of this world, just as God said it would. Free gift, without price, lavishly bestowed upon you and I. He gives all, we give nothing.

Yes, our lives should be changed; our actions altered in conformance to His perfect will, but never as an attempt to earn it. We are changed because of His love for us, and readily conform because of our love for Him. Our deeds are not payment; they are in service to the one we love, just because we love. We reach out because He asks it of us, not because we must in order to be saved.

I have been saved from this life of death. You have been saved from this life of death. All He wants is to help us live in the fullness of this wondrous eternal life with which he has gifted us.

What a wonderful, wonderful, Savior.

Yes...

You can still get something for nothing...

Nothing To Offer

I have nothing, Lord, to offer You.
My hands are empty.
Anything I might ever attain would be as nothing before You.
I try and try to be good,
To reach the point of miserably less than perfect,
Only to find that I am miles away from even that poor measure.

I have nothing, Lord, to offer You.
I wonder at times if You did not look closely enough...
before choosing me.
Yes, Father, I know nothing eludes You,
Still, at the risk of belligerence, may I please ask why me?
Did You see something in me that I have yet to see?

I have nothing, Lord, to offer You.
My faith weakens when provoked,
My hands fail to perform the most menial of tasks when prompted.
I see all of the wondrous works You do through others,
What have I to give My Master in return for this good fortune?
How can I repay what I do not understand?
Father, I am bowed by the awesome grace I have received.

I have nothing, Lord, to offer You.
This, then, I suppose, must be what I offer...
Nothing...
Nothing of the old me that wallowed in pride and pity,
Nothing of the shell that purposed to find her own way in this world,
Nothing of the shadow I used to be.
Nothing of the faithless, angry creation I was before you found me.
Oh Lord, I have nothing to offer You,
Please receive my nothing and make it something in Your hands.

Clean Slate

A blackboard set before me,
Satan scribbles every sin
Highlighting retched moments,
When victory fell to him.

A mocking laugh upon his lips,
His hands twisting in glee,
Writing, writing, never rest,
His words accusing me.

Remember this one, little fool
Oh, you are bad indeed
And this one, here, gnarled finger points
Yes, this one planted seeds

See your life, pitiful you,
You'll never get it right,
Oh, look right here, "warrior"
You didn't even fight.

Come a splintering of wood,
Classroom door falls to the ground
Booming voice fair shakes the walls
A roaring outraged sound

How dare you assume to speak!
This one belongs to Me.
Be gone foul One, your works undone,
Come, small one, you will see

Before my very eyes,
Accusing words began to fade,
His breath upon the board,
Erased mistakes that I had made.

Each and every vile thing
The creature had thrown at me,
Covered by a crimson flow,
That brought me to my knee.

Gratitude overwhelmed me,
As His hand lay on my head,
Your past can be a jailer, child,
Let love free you instead.

I turned to look upon the boards,
My heart did melt within,
For written in that crimson flow...
My child, begin again...

And finally,
If I may,
I will close with the songs of my heart...

Secret Pastures

Lord, You awaken me in night watches,
Bidding me to come and play
Your precious perfume lingers,
my breath catches
As You call love, come away

Come to the secret pastures
The place where you and I alone can dwell
Love in these secret pastures
You will know Me well

Have you seen my Fair One,
my beautiful love?
The One my heart does long to know?
His touch is like no other,
He calls me His small one
I have to tell Him I need Him so,

Come to the secret pastures
The place where you and I alone can dwell
Love in these secret pastures
You will know Me well

Oh, come and sit beside Me,
I've a story to tell
One of love unparalleled
It started in the beginning
and still burns today

Sweet Beloved,
Sweet Beloved,
Come away

A Bride's Song

My gaze is fixed on You
My Arms are wide open too
It's what any good bride would do
When her Bridegroom comes into the room

I'm captivated, enthralled by You
I have waited, keeping my heart true
How I've longed for this time with You

In this Holy place
I know the sweetness of Your embrace
The Sacred secrets of Your lovely face
Oh, Bridegroom come into the room

I'm captivated, enthralled by You
I have waited, keeping my heart true
How I've longed for this time with You

So soft your voice I hear
Fragrance surrounds me, as You draw near
My heart quickens, it seems so clear
When my Bridegroom comes into the room.

I'm captivated, enthralled by You
I have waited, keeping my heart true
How I've longed for this time with You

My gaze is fixed on You
My Arms are wide open too
It's what any good bride would do
When her Bridegroom comes into the room

Swept Away

My feet now wet upon this shore
A cry from my heart torn
My face into the wind my arms outstretched
Embracing more
And in this sacred moment
I am swept away

His Spirit hovers
O'er these waters
Creation moves through me
Beneath the waves, I know His voice
His Words they beckon me
And in this sacred moment
I am swept away

Be still my heart
Stir up, O' soul
Swift plunge into the deep
In crashing wave, sweet refuge find
New water's rhythm keep
For one sacred moment
Be swept away

Beautiful You Are

Beautiful You Are—The Dream

The room was quiet as I drew the covers up to my chin. My mother, whom I was visiting at the time, loves to keep the house cold at night so I burrowed deeper in to the downy blankets as my mind began to drift into the soft recesses of semi-consciousness. I remember thinking, *God, You are so beautiful to me... beautiful, You are so beautiful.* As my eyes closed and sleep came, my spirit man soared and completely explored what my conscious mind could not. I journeyed into the fierce beauty of God.

This is my testimony.

I stood as an onlooker... a silent witness to the sacred goings on around me. I knew that I slept, but at the same time knew that what I was seeing was very real; more tangible than the touchable and more fluid than water through the fingers.

The expanse of space before my eyes was completely white, yet shape and shadow, form and movement could be easily seen, or perhaps a better word would be sensed. I had a keen awareness of the center point from which all flowed in this place—life, breath, wholeness...joy. I knew without anyone telling me that the place I stood within was Holy, yet completely accessible. There was

Sovereignty in communion with fragile humanity. To describe the scene in fleshly terms falls pitifully short of the profoundly peaceful, exquisitely detailed perfection of the atmosphere in which I found myself.

The Throne sat in the center of the space. I could not see it, though I knew it was directly to my right. I knew He sat upon it… though I could not see Him. I looked directly into the place in which I knew Him to be, still, my eyes were unable to see His beauty. I found Him beautiful, nonetheless. The very breathe of God filled the room with piercing clarity and reverent awe.

How can I explain what I knew, but could not see? How does one give a description of spiritual sights they did not see, but saw nonetheless?

Just as the Throne sat within the center of the space, white, yet translucent; without actual substance, but substantial all the same, so did the crowd surround the Throne. For defining purposes I will call them the cloud of witnesses. Beginning at a circumference of about 100 feet and spreading for as far as the eyes could see, this invisible, present throng stood silent, yet their praise was felt through every fiber of my being. They encompassed a limitless space, circling the unseen but known.

I watched as one mesmerized as one small person emerged from the crowd. Walking forward, head bowed, the small one approached the foot of the Throne and the One Who sat upon it. I could see that the small one held something within her hands; something which she longed to lay at the feet of The Holy One. She beheld the gift as if it might not be enough, and struggled with the releasing of it because of its smallness. The desire to give was greater than the gift she was able to bring. Still, she offered it with words I could not hear, from a heart that sang in worship to Him Who sat upon the Throne. As the gift touched the feet of God, the eyes of the giver lifted to the One Who received. An absolute liquid radiance filled her face as she beheld Him and she began to sing to the Father…

Beautiful, You are… Beautiful, You are… Beautiful, You are, to me…
The crowd began to sing the song as if they had sung it for ages; their voices lifting in sweet unison with the small one… *Beautiful, You are, Beautiful, You are. Beautiful, You are to me.*

The One Who sat upon the Throne accepted the gift and the worship and He was pleased. Fulfillment, unequaled, poured through the small one as she gazed upon her Beloved. She rose slowly, eyes fixed upon Him, and began to walk away; her face turned toward Him, looking back over her shoulder as she walked… gazing upon a visage I as yet, had not been able to look upon.

I wondered what gift she had offered. Just as the thought ran through my mind, I knew the answer: *"All she had."*

My heart pounded as I watched to see what would happen next. Again, I watched one leave the crowd and walk forward, hands cupped as if carrying an offering. This one walked as if wounded. His legs did not move as one in good health. Haltingly he approached, his gaze turned downward. Before He reached the feet of the Holy One, he stumbled and fell. As he fell, he made no move to catch himself, but instead, released the offering toward the feet of God. Facedown he lay, his offering tumbling over the feet of Holiness. As the simple offering touched the holy, strength came into the man and he rose to hands and knees. He sat back upon his heels and gazed for the first time into the face of the Holy One. Falling forward, this time of reverent awe, I heard the smallest sound begin to come from the lips of the man – words I could not hear, but understood. Then, just as the small one had done, he began to sing: *Beautiful… Beautiful… Beautiful, You are Beautiful.*

The throng joined in the awed chorus, testimonies acknowledging what their spirits knew full well… *Beautiful, You are… Beautiful, You are…*

When I looked again upon the man, he stood full height and strong backed. Muscle and sinew had formed upon what had once been weakened flesh. His voice strong now, he sang in a rich baritone, issuing forth from a deep well… *Beautiful, You are…*

Turning, he began to walk the way of the first, turning to glance over His shoulder at The One. Whole now, I could not stop the thought, *What did he bring, Lord?*

Again, I knew the answer before speaking, *"The rest".*

I had no need to ask what He meant, for I have all too often heard the words of the Spirit within speaking those same words to me... *What about the rest?*

Finally, I watched as what appeared to be a beautiful woman, separated herself from the cloud of witnesses. Walking forward, her gaze was fixed upon Him from the very first moment she stepped out. She knew Him well. He had truly captivated her heart. She moved with a graceful rhythm to her step, almost dancing as she brought her offering. Her eyes never left His until the moment she stood at His feet. Without hesitation she fell to her knees, her arms coming around His ankles as her tears flowed over His feet. Her face resting against his calve, His garment came around her shoulders. He covered her, for He was her Kinsman Redeemer. Her tears mingled with the offering of fragrant oil she held in her hand. She began to pour the oil over His feet. The small vile became an endless supply, and its fragrance began to fill the nostrils of the masses. The woman bent forward, kissed the top of each foot and resumed her enveloped place at His feet. With tears streaming down her face, dampening the precious Kinsman garment with which He had covered her, she began to sing, *Beautiful, You are... Beautiful, You are..., Beautiful, You are to me...*

The oil pooled and gathered, increased and began to flow. Tears and fragrant oil began to reach the feet of the throng, and they began to sing full voiced. *Beautiful, You are...*

Lord, I thought, what did she bring? What could have possibly brought that would release the throng in this way? I simply heard, *"Her testimony."*

I knew He spoke of her love for Him. It was her testimony. It was who she had become in Him. She was His, and the testimony of this redemption was great.

As the space filled with the purest expression of what I can only describe as the wetness of worship, the cloud of witnesses began to sing their own testimony. Each testimony was different, but as it issued from their lips, the song became the same... *Beautiful, You are...*

In this moment of acute awareness the unseen somehow became visible, and faith became sight. The room filled with His presence and His fragrance became a part of me.

Without seeing, I saw, and without touching, I felt, and the song began to rise within me. I heard myself singing, as my spirit stood witness to the offerings of thousands, and I knew for certain what I had always thought I'd known... He is Beautiful: Fiercely, marvelously, beautiful. He is unparalleled in every imaginable way.

The sound of my voice awakened me in my mother's house, as I sang aloud the chorus of heaven. I could not shake the changeless rhythm of it. I reached for a pen and wrote down the words I had heard.

For weeks I carried the song of the witnesses. Everywhere I went I moved with its rhythm. I could not come out of that place. It moved within me like a living thing, this "worship that sees." Finally, one day as I sat pondering the song within, understanding dawned. I am not supposed to lose their song and move forward. I am supposed to take their song forward. I am supposed to carry the song of the witness, sharing the knowledge that they have gained with the ones who seek this wisdom in the earth, until all come to the deep understanding of His Fierce Beauty, and can sing with one voice... *Beautiful, You are. Beautiful, You are. Beautiful, You are to me...*

And the cloud of witnesses joins the song...

Beautiful, You Are—The Song

I will not offer You
That which costs me nothing
I will not come before You
with empty hands
This fragrant oil of worship
I will lavish upon You
As I bow at the feet of my Holy God

Beautiful, You are
Beautiful You are
Beautiful You are, to me

I lift my cup to You
Give it all up for You
Lay everything out before Your eyes
Everything that I should be
Could or would be
I leave at the feet of my Holy God

Beautiful, You are
Beautiful You are
Beautiful You are, to me

Oh, My Kinsman Redeemer
May your handmaiden draw near
Spread Your garment over me a while
For Your song it does call me,
As this threshing floor draws me
To lay at the feet of my Holy God

Beautiful, You are
Beautiful You are
Beautiful You are, to me

*T*o find a place to end this pouring out of spirit matters is virtually impossible to a heart that would love to continue the journey.

So, I simply lay down my pen... knowing He will allow me to pick it up again, soon.

It is my sincere prayer that we never stop learning, never cease living with great passion for Our Beloved, and that we always seek to see this world through His eyes.

Our Precious Father has so very much in store for His children. May we press ever forward, until we reach the place where His perfect will is all that we desire.

May our lives be ever Poured Out

For the sake of His Name

Barbie

www.ingramcontent.com/pod-product-compliance
Lightning Source LLC
Chambersburg PA
CBHW071013120626
46546CB00003B/1065